This is a journey into, through and out of the human condition, hand-in-hand with a man who's willing to share it all with you. Such loneliness, such arrow-to-the-heart-ness, such clear-eyed-Harlem-Globetrotting-languageful-playfulness. Dan is a note-taking naturalist tiptoeing through the landscape of the human heart. Each one of his book-projects is special in a new way, and this one does not disappoint in the slightest.

A.F. Harrold

I dare you to read this book aloud and not stop. To confront ten years of personal and cultural devastation. Dan speaks to us through us. All characters of the universe are present in these poems, thoughts and questionnaires, those we know intimately and those who don't want to know us at all. Inspiration and associations with concepts far bigger than us drip through in the crush of sound, and turns of phrases and personal notes for context. A constant wrestle with hypocrisy and destruction. Loneliness is an internal terrorism. Notes on Loneliness is an acknowledgement and truce with our other self.

Deanna Rodger

Also by Daniel Cockrill

Pie And Papier-Mâché

Mud Wrestling With Words / Bang Said The Gun Anthology

Sellotaping Rain To My Cheek

Destroying The Laboratory For The Sake Of The Experiment

In The Beginning Was The Word, Then A Drawing, Then More
Words, Another Drawing, And So On And So On

Daniel Cockrill's words have appeared in books, newspapers, magazines, on gallery walls and have been spoken out loud on stage, radio and television. He is the co-founder of Bang Said The Gun and Page Match. He lives and works in London.

www.danielcockrill.com

Notes On Loneliness

Daniel Cockrill

Illustrations by

Damien Weighill

Burning Eye

This edition published by Burning Eye Books 2019

www.burningeye.co.uk

@burningeyebooks

Burning Eye Books
15 West Hill, Portishead, BS20 6LG

ISBN 978-1-911570-73-8

I wrote this book for the lonely and for you to know that you are not alone in our shared sadness.

This book is to be read out loud.

Contents

"DID YOU EVER SEE A ROBIN WEEP
WHEN LEAVES BEGAN TO DIE?
LIKE ME, HE'S LOST THE WILL TO LIVE
I'M SO LONESOME I COULD CRY."
Hank Williams

"I used to think the worst thing in life is to end up all alone. It's not. The worst thing in life is to end up with people who make you feel all alone."
- Robin Williams

'Notes on Loneliness' is a collection of commissioned, unpublished and new writing between 2007 - 2018.

During the process of writing this book, I imagined I was a butterfly dancing to the slowest and sweetest song ever played on a piano, similar to the way raindrops fall from petals in gentle rain, or like an astronaut floating through space, travelling about the speed of the boat on a Disney World ride, the one where you get to see all the places in the world in about fifteen minutes, but instead of visiting well-known landmarks, I imagined myself visiting different planets and distant stars, trying to figure out where I fitted in, whilst looking back at my family and friends on Earth, trying to remember who they were, what they looked like, and asking questions like 'did I really know them?' or 'do I really need them?' or 'how fast do asteroids travel?' or 'why is gravity?' as I travelled away from them in space.

Here on Earth, I have a loving family, a good home life, lots of very good friends; I have everything I could possibly need and yet I still feel lonely. This book is an attempt to discover why.

Things To Consider When Writing A Book About Loneliness

What is the loneliest planet in the universe?

What is the loneliest star?

What is the loneliest number?

What is the loneliest cheese?

What is the loneliest fruit?

What is the loneliest animal on Earth?

What is the loneliest road in London?

What is the loneliest place on the planet?

What is the loneliest country in the world?

What is the loneliest day of the year?

What is the loneliest day of the week?

What is the loneliest day ever recorded?

Who are the loneliest age group? It's probably not who you immediately think.

What is the loneliest song ever sung?

What is the loneliest job in the world?

What is the loneliest thing you have ever done?

What is the loneliest you've ever felt?

What is the loneliest idea?

What is the loneliest question ever asked?

What is the loneliest feeling someone has ever felt?

Who had the loneliest ever thought?

Is the person who had the loneliest thought the same person who had the loneliest feeling ever felt?

Who is the loneliest person in the world?

Is the loneliest person in the world the same person who had the loneliest thought or the loneliest feeling?

Who is the loneliest monk?

Who is the loneliest child?

Who is the loneliest ruler?

Who is the loneliest superhero?

Who is the loneliest whale?

Who is the loneliest orangutan?

Who is the loneliest human?

Who is the loneliest?

What is the loneliest?

What is lonely?

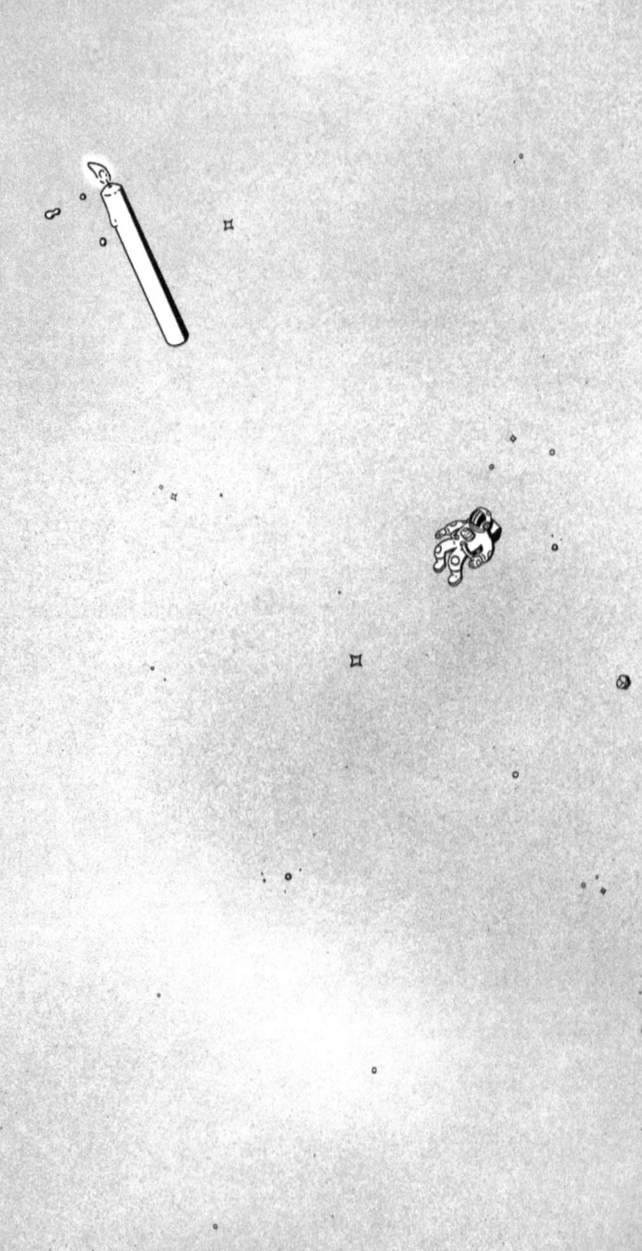

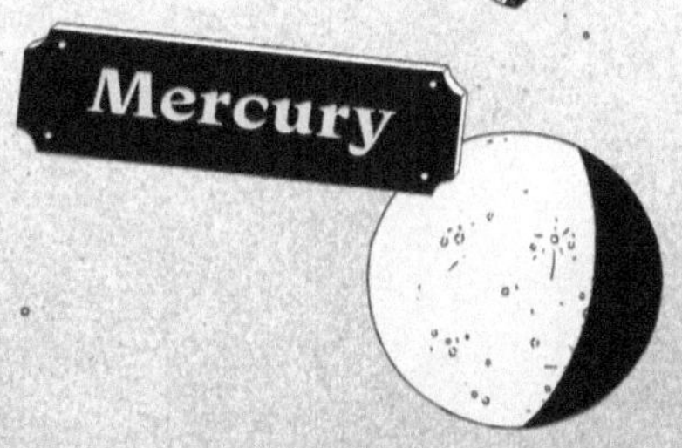
Mercury

What Is Emptiness?

You can almost see the tears as old as his eyes falling from mantels / Tears that hold wisdom the size of blue whales / They've memorised books and songs and stories in their bottomless bellies / Lit with the light of a single candle / The corridors like orchards with white dust-covered apples / Or night-time vineyards with tall vines reaching high to heavy skies / The mead and cider barrels have been drunk dry.

What is emptiness?

When no light is let in / When the shutter is closed / Or the way night falls like a bucket into a bottomless well / The shelves are full of longing for another era like a silent swarm of yesterdays / Silk moths standing in line awaiting death / Perfectly formed / Keeping their outer shape / But their insides disintegrate before they reach the front of the queue.

The security man is just doing his job / Guarding the decay / "They're thinking of bringing in CCTV" he says / "I'm not quite sure how that will affect us" / But he is sure / He has seen the thick layer of dust appear on the wooden floor / The padlocked door / The redundant lazy broom / The faded laminate / The kettle and pot and black / The ripple and corrugated clad building / The council office looming / Over wasted ground and wasted lives and wasted ware / And tear and tears and taps are locked off till water runs dry.

The rough and the rust / The grit and the bit between teeth / The quit / It's all gone to pot / The rotting knotty deck / The unkept unswept dusty stair / The cupboard bare / The shutdown shutter / The unquestioning runner / Moulds discarded / Workers disregarded / A hollow ceramic dinosaur bone fossil thought / Excavate a memory / Etch and engrave into the distant traffic drone / The moan and bone rattle / And bone shaker bicycle / And bone china / And china plate / Through iron gate / Nose to the grindstone / To tombstone / And ghost town / Burn it down / With furnace and fire / Bone in and trim / Cottle up and size up / Cast wax and resin / Biscuit and blocker / Lime slip and water / Scooped dipped stamped / Fettle cast pack mark and fold / Burnishing gold.

Moulds like moon craters / Eyes like telescopes / Dust-caked / Face cracked / Scratches of tiger-stripe light in long grass / Reveal rickety and nervous shelves / They do not look up to the job of holding up the years / The weight of which could crush lungs / Break backs / The strain buckling legs as if cradling uranium dreams / But the shelves stand strong like a ceramic St Christopher / The weight of Jesus Christ on his twisted back / At risk of sinking beneath the soft clay bed into underwater arms / Pulled tight into a dead man's chest / Sealed oyster shell shut.

If the moulds could speak their solitude would weep / Three-hundred-year-old stories / Spin yarns on a potter's wheel past /

But those tales are locked in / Tomblike / Mouths stitched / Sewn shut / Vocal cords slit cut / Never to be spoken / White flowers in snow-covered dark rooms / The light is old and ancient like waves that have travelled a long distance / Their destination is the shoreline but they've lost their way over time / The perpetual wave break an unending bereavement like widows in darkness.

Even though we are present / Here / Now / There is a distance in this room / The space between is a mountain range / Untouchable / Unreachable / Over the horizon / Its very being seems impossible / Existing in a very far-off land / In a coma / It is here but not here / In a dream state / Between here and heaven / Keeping secrets alive on a life support machine / These shelves a preserved state of loss / The body here / The spirit elsewhere / The here of this place is elsewhere.

Invisible and unspoken / An almost unexplainable love / It is love / Battered love / Broken love / Shattered love / Shrapnel blast love / The absence of love / The absence of care / Something that disappears before your lover's eyes / An hallucination as if trapped in a conjurer's trick gone wrong / Moulds sitting like fatigued travellers / Thirsting for liquid plaster to be poured in their vents / Glimpsing a mirage in the distant desert / This place is an illusion.

But these words are proof / A record of a vast chamber of loss / The fracture of manufacturing / An eternal task to preserve their Sisyphus state / Too little too late / This is their fate / This is emptiness.

We Didn't Know It Was Called Hip-Hop (Part 1)

We didn't know it was called hip-hop.

To us it was rap music or break dance / It was all caterpillars / Windmills and knee spins / If you were athletic then you'd attempt a head spin / But I stuck to my knees burning holes in my Tarahs / Yeah Tarahs / We were poor enough that my mum couldn't afford Farah trousers / But we still considered ourselves casuals / We wore the fashion of football thugs / In our mock-West-Ham-Inter-City-Firm clobber / I had no idea what it meant / All I remember was that Micky Adler's dad had a white hooded suit hanging in his wardrobe / And he burnt crosses on the hill across the estuary / When you are ten you don't feel scared about things you don't understand / I stare at Micky and tell him I want to be Mr T from the A-Team / This throws him for about twenty minutes / In which time he has decided to get his mates to beat me up everyday after school for a month / I suppose this is really the only time I've experienced racism / There were no black people where I lived / So they decided to beat up a kid who fantasised about being Mr T / I don't let the bullying put me off / I tell my mum that I want to be Mr T / I don't tell her about the bullying / Before I know it I'm asking my mum for a gold chain for Christmas / And she looks at me as if to say / "You'd be wearing Farahs if we could afford gold, you crazy fool!"

I swap my West Ham shirt for an Arsenal shirt underneath

the lamp post outside our house / My dad stops speaking to me and listening to me / He has never seen me perform poetry.

Hip-hop is my first date to the cinema / I don't fancy her / She smells funny drenched in her mum's cheap perfume / But the thought of it is exciting / The film is *Breakin'* / "Push it to pop it! Rock it to lock it! Break it to make it!"/ I'm not sure what the tagline is trying to tell me / I'm eleven and on my first date / "Break it to make it?"

Hip-hop to me was *Beat Street* / *Turk 182* / *Electric Boogaloo* / Kid 'n Play's *House Party* / Roxanne Shante / *Street Sounds Electro 6* / And as I attempt a back spin / I look up at the cracked ceiling / And realise at an early age that Artex looks ridiculous.

Then rewind / Click / Play / And the beat kicks in / I look over at the ghetto blaster / Well, we're calling it a ghetto blaster / But it's actually a little black tape recorder with one speaker / But we're carrying it like it's a ghetto blaster / And we're walking with it on our shoulder like it's a ghetto blaster / Stuffed full with super-sized batteries (the really big ones) / So it's a ghetto blaster, right, you get me!

We know what a ghetto blaster is / We don't know what a ghetto is / And we don't question it.

The sun's out / My brother shouts / "Let's do it in the street where real breakers do battle!" / But we're just working-class white kids / With working-class holes in our trousers / "And we've got no lino" I reply.

He grabs the knife from Dad's tool box / Cuts the lino from the kitchen floor revealing chipboard below / Six to eight square feet / Big enough for some white boy windmill action / We are overcome / Mum's wrath is hours and miles from our thoughts.

As Kraftwerk Tour de France makes minds drift / To the scene where Turbo hovers with broom on street corner / This is categorically the only time I can remember that I feel lucky that my dad is a cleaner / We scoot to the garage / Grab three or four brooms / And skate around lino like street dance Torvill and Deans / The Bolero beating we took on our sunburnt backs was worth every strike of the hand / The stinging sensation / And the shower warming tight red skin / Is still a thrill in my memory.

2007 / I'm in Chicago / I'm shaking Kool Herc's hand / And I'm like / "This guy invented the biggest subculture on the entire planet by spinning records at his big sister's house parties" / So big / That when I was a small boy / It came down my quiet Essex street / Into my bedroom / Infected my best friends / And our souls / And we didn't even realise it / And it helped me break free to discover this new spoken-word-hip-hop-rap-poetry / The stuff that fights homophobia / Racism / Misogyny / Fights for fairness / And it thrills me / And I love it / And I'm in love with it.

See / My generation are from hip-hop / I'm from hip-hop / I'm from milk tokens and poverty / Hand-me-downs / I'm from working class / I'm from too-proud-to-claim-social-benefit-or-the-neighbours-will-talk / I'm from you've-got-ideas-above-your-station-son / Simmer down / Button up / Put a sock in it / I'm from we-don't-want-any-of-that-foreign-muck / The latent unsaid racism / That sometimes spills over and reveals itself through violence / I'm from patriotic tattoos / And the worship of Union Flags / I'm from "What you looking at? I'll wipe that smile off your face!" / Where lips forever blow bubbles / Where those bubbles turn into dreams that fade and die.

You ask me what I'm doing now / And why I didn't stay / I say / Read the above.

We Didn't Know It Was Called Hip-Hop (Part 2)

Melancholy lasted forever in those open spaces / Because it had no walls / Or backboards / Or break beats to bounce off / It just kept on rolling for miles and miles / Where it would eventually melt over the horizon and fade into depression or anxiety / We could see our future in front of us / And there was nothing there / Just open fields.

You can out-sprint melancholy but you can't outrun it / It will just keep on going like a long-distance runner / Tracking your every move / Tracing your every step / Sniffing your scent like a dog over every hill / Every river you have ever crossed / Until it finds you / Broken / Exhausted.

Mrs Earl / My English teacher / Kept me behind after class to tell me that she fancied my dad / Mrs Mundane / My media studies teacher / Used to massage my head in class / But the one that affected me most was Mrs Rumpus / My science teacher / And careers advisor / She asked me what I wanted to be when I left school / And I said, "I want to be an artist."

I'm still unsure what she meant by her reply / "You have to be good to be an artist" / Did she mean I had to be a good person? / Or did she mean I had to be a good artist? / I was fourteen / My dad was a window cleaner / And my mum made television aerials in the local factory / Books and words were in short supply / *Know your place, son,* is what I took from her cryptic message / She promptly quashed my dreams in one blow by directing me to a page in the beaten-up job folder / Showing the address for the local garden centre and building merchants.

We've had loads of good ideas stolen from us / But we're working class / That's what's meant to happen / Start on the back foot / Get a good kicking whilst you are down / And then step up to the white line with the rest of them / To prove yourself with your beaten-down spirit / When you keep looking up and losing / Your confidence has no time to recover / You feel failure / You are failure / As Mrs Rumpus implied / You are no good / This feeling still hurts / It's like going up against Usain Bolt / And he gets a fifty-metre head start / Go on – go catch him! / Except in this case Usain Bolt is an over-privileged white male / Probably driving a golf cart / And saying "It's okay, it's in the rules. Come on, try and catch me!"

Poverty never leaves you / You never quite forget it / It's a heavy load / A blister on your heel / It's an uncomfortable pain in your gut when you are sipping wine and eating steak in Shoreditch House / It's a nagging / A finger prodding / A reminder of where you are from.

I never quite got over the mundanity of it all / The bungalows / The bricks and the mortar / The low boredom threshold / The smell of pot wafting from windows / Teenage girls sucking on fags at graffiti-tagged broken-down bus stops / Blowing out their dreams with every puff / Kids kicking footballs against kerbs / Older kids kicking heads against pavement / It all kicking off after midnight kick-out / I just never got used to it / I feel the same way now as I did when I was fourteen / The end of summer days / The loneliness / The memories and melancholy are written on the inside of my eyelids.

Take a close look.

I'm a dad / These days I go to parent-toddler groups / The only thing we have in common is the fact we all have kids / It's like hanging out with people from a self-harm group because you share the same scars / Getting inside people's minds doesn't win their hearts.

Hip-hop was stolen from you / From us / From my generation early on / But it didn't crush our spirit / The same way universities steal and intellectualise all the best ideas / Or the way real estate buys up all the best houses / You can live in a box and still make it feel like home / Because you fill it with love / Whereas the mansions are cold / Empty / Sterile / Sad / Lonely / Like the world trending latest hip-hop music video / It's all gloss and vacuous / An empty vessel.

Converse All Stars with no Larry Bird shooting over the backboard at the buzzer / Air Jordan 3s with no Michael

dunking from the free-throw line / Just shoes / Laces tied /
Hung over telephone wires / With no one to fill them.

But you have to be empty / Like an empty cup / So that you
can be filled.

Keep your ideas on the street / In the back room / In the
basement / Spray-painted tag tattoos on whitewashed walls /
Keep your ideas underground for as long as you possibly can /
Don't be tempted to take the quick buck / Once you lose it /
Once you give it away / Or sell your gifts for cheap / You may
never get it back.

The Road To Wigan Casino

pass through arched canal path
warehouse and wharf
pit shaft and mill town
burn it down

suck in smoke choked filled
Sunday morning amphetamine-fuelled
rhythm and blue hue
seven days is too long without you

two quid in
rare disc demo spin
no moonshine no firewater no alcohol
just guts dance and Northern soul

two-tone Spencer peg clobber
twisted industrial youth truth
as you flip-kick backdrop
to knees and pray

as Dean Parrish sings
I'm on my way

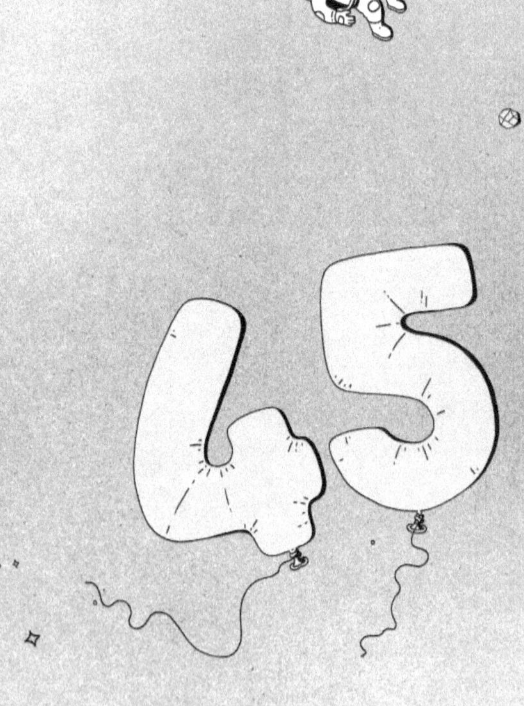

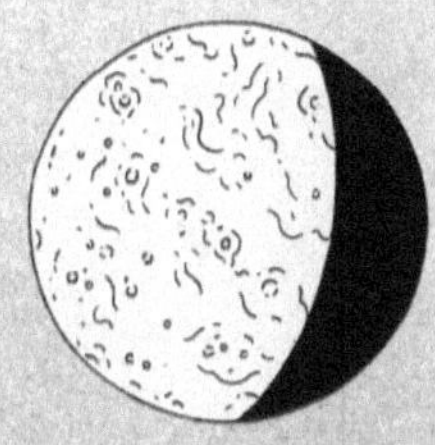

Venus

what if I loved you like sunlight dripping through the window

When My World Was Turned

upside down
everything fell out

in the morning
I fell out of bed

my pens fell out my bag
my money fell out my pocket
my tears fell out my eyes
my thoughts fell out my ears
my anger fell out my mouth
my hate fell out my fists
my love fell out my heart
my heart fell out my chest

luckily
you walked behind me
and picked them all up

Double Ectopic

when you disappeared
behind the surgery door
I waited for you to come back
but you never really came back

Man In Pub Asking Another Man In Pub This Question:

Do you believe in love?

Well / I believe in stardust and chemistry / And souls and the unknown / And life on distant planets / I probably don't believe in humans as much as I used to / I feel disappointed with myself for that / I should probably try harder when it comes to other humans / If I see a shooting star I wish on it / And deep down I believe in magic and the universe / And if I mix up all of those things / And see us and the whole thing as a work in progress / The imperfections become absolutely perfect / And because of that / I guess I believe in love.

Love is...

a)   an espresso shot of stupidity ☐

b)   being blinded by a violent darkness whilst being set upon by dogs ☐

c)   tiny continents like a butterfly wing beat washing waves upon a silent shore ☐

d)   an exchanged item from the supermarket delivery van that is nothing like the thing you ordered ☐

e)   a small five-year-old boy asking, "Why is gravity?" and "Do worms know when it is time to go to bed?" ☐

f)   none of the above ☐

g)   all of the above ☐

She Cried Crushed Apples

I talk to your eyes
and when they are drunk
they are gone

*My wife used to work in fashion and as a consequence is really
good at dressing people and folding clothes. She is now a midwife
and delivers neatly folded babies into the arms of their mother.*

you dress like the solar system
your clothed planets swirling perfectly round your blazing body
comets shooting from your eyes and hitting my dead moon soul
your thoughts spinning like satellites through your ears and
out your mouth
like distant radio signals from another galaxy
and my words find you and fall like black holes
as I sit back and watch the seasons fold and twist around you
like playing cards

Sunday was a perfect day / We walked hand in hand through the flower market / Haggled for herbs / And splashed out on your favourite / A Bougainvillea / Your mum said not to bother because it will only die / She was right / Yet we bought it anyway / And planted it in a pot that was far too small for its advanced roots / Our first feeble attempt at gardening / Our first garden / Ours / Mine and yours / You and me / Last Sunday / A perfect day.

because I'm in love with the world
everybody can come for a ride in my spaceship

For my birthday I want a huge number forty-five silver balloon /
A balloon bigger than the Earth / With string long enough to tie
around the equator / So the balloon will float above the world /
And everyone will know that it is my birthday / "Ah look, it's
Dan's birthday, he's tied a balloon around the world" / The
world would then unite in singing me Happy Birthday / And I
will blow my candles out to the words / "Make a wish."

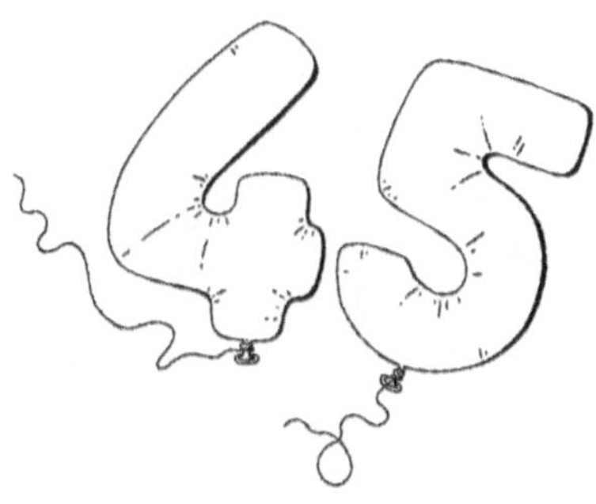

All Light Creates Shadows Even If The Darkness Falls Underground

every part of you
that came from a dead star is alive again
and asks questions like
why is gravity?

Earth

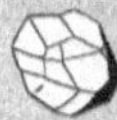

I Sit Them On The Wall

two boys
outside my house
facing the busy street
their backs pressed against my chest
the sensation is the closest thing I know to magic

a lone man walks past

they point, smile and wave
"hello"
the lone man smiles and waves back
an action I'm not sure he would usually do

"bye bye" they say and wave "bye bye"

a mother and her little girl walk past

two boys
backs pressed against my chest
point, smile and wave
"hello"
the mother and her little girl smile and wave back
"look, two babies" says the little girl

"bye bye" they say and wave "bye bye"

a group of boys with baggy uniform and a headphone limp
walk past

two boys
backs pressed tightly against my chest
point, smile and wave
"hello"
the group smile and wave back
"dem cute"

"bye bye" they say and wave "bye bye"

a white van man with tattoos on his neck and face drives past

two boys
backs pressed tightly against my chest
they point, smile and wave
"hello"
the white van man smiles and waves back
and lets out a cheer from out his open window

"bye bye" they say and wave "bye bye"

the single-decker bus drives past

two boys
backs pressed tightly against my chest
they point, smile and wave
"hello"

the bus driver smiles and waves back

the bus stops in traffic

the two boys point, smile and wave
to all the passengers on the bus
"hello"

soon everybody is smiling and waving
the whole bus is smiling and waving
everybody that walks past is smiling and waving

and in that moment I try to remember
why we stopped pointing and smiling and waving

and I think it's because we are told pointing is rude
so we stop pointing
and we stop staring
and looking at each other
and we stop smiling and waving
and communicating
and we become sad

and in that moment I become sad

imagine if my arms were empty

Dad, have the robots reached the sun yet?

my boys are learning to read on the train as we pull into
Reading station
"It says Reading Daddy, Reading station"
"Yes it does, well done, good reading"
then the woman on the seat opposite chips in and says
"It is actually pronounced Reading"
and I cut her a stare capable of wounding
and declare
"Don't listen to her lies boys
it's Reading station
a station for reading
where people go to read"

I Love You Like The Universe When You Climb Into My Bed In The Morning

the stars spread out like fingers on your ever-expanding palm
which you place gently on my weathered cheek
as you speak in whispered phonic beats
"d d d d d" "p p p p p"
as you practise your letter sounds
and recognise words
that you begin to read
in your wildest dreams

Your handwriting reflects your personality / Finn is five and his handwriting is very precise and neat / People comment on how good his handwriting is / Bill is Finn's twin brother / His handwriting is big and bold / No one comments on how good his handwriting is / They both have amazing handwriting / This is how you should approach life / The way you do things is amazing / You are amazing / I don't want you to change / I don't want you to change your handwriting.

Children are...

a)   the disturbed dust floating in a beam of
     sunlight ☐

b)   a really clean, almost invisible window that
     a fledgling bird mistakes as a gap ☐

c)   the disrupters of thoughts ☐

d)   a visit to the supermarket with no reusable bags ☐

e)   a pool of freezing water that has forgotten how
     to be ice ☐

f)   none of the above ☐

g)   all of the above ☐

Infinity x Infinity x Infinity

"Dad, what's infinity times infinity times infinity?"

"Erm, not sure, I think it's infinity."

"Dad, what is the biggest number in the world?"

"Erm, I don't know that either."

"What do you mean? You've been here for so many years
  and you still do not know the biggest number in the world?"

"Err, no."

"Why don't you just gurgle it?"

Conversation With Bill After Edging The Cricket Ball Into A Hedge

"We can never play cricket again" he said, head down.

"What never?"

"No, never again."

"Why? We could just buy another ball."

"But we will lose that ball too, and we will keep on losing
the balls, and then all the balls in the world will be lost.
So we can never play cricket ever again."

Football Is As Interesting As A Renaissance Painting To A Five-Year-Old

I show off my mediocre ball skills in the garden
"I'll be in goal," Billy says
"Try and score against me"
I dribble and pretend I've given a world-class defender the slip
with my style and grace
I turn and shoot!
The ball hits Billy in the chest
"I'm not playing anymore," he says
"I want to play something else that hasn't been invented yet"

There are many Germans on the campsite / The children are playing football / Even at this early age they are already more technically gifted than the English children / Finn who is five is playing with the older children / Some more than twice his age / The older German kids are impressed with his skill and speed / The older boy keeps saying, "Schön, schön," when Finn is on the ball / And one of the other German boys says, "You are a sports rocket," in his broken English / Which I think is 'very gut'.

Me: Bill, what's your favourite animal?
Bill: A potato

"Where did the rainbow go?" he said.

"I don't know, son, it just disappeared."

"Will it come back?"

"I guess so, one day."

"Are rainbows real, Dad?"

"I'm not sure anymore. I thought they were but I'm not sure. Rainbows are like hope; you think you can see it, but most of the time there's nothing concrete to hold on to. It's just an illusion of the light."

Billy Draws Treasure Maps

Billy likes to draw treasure maps
he has drawn hundreds and hundreds of them
and one day he will draw a treasure map that will lead him to
the secret treasure

If you follow my wife's family history back far enough, her family tree can be traced to Thomas Bates, one of the members of the infamous Gunpowder Plot. I have twin boys. Finn, the younger twin, has the middle names Thomas Bates. By sheer coincidence, my twin boys were born on November 5th. Maybe one day Finn Thomas Bates will find it within himself to bring down Parliament using gunpowder and fireworks.

November 5th Is Over

bonfire
gone fire

Bus Stop

Mars

The Movie

let's write a two-line poem
and get Hollywood to make a movie about it

before they were stars they were a cloud of dust and gas
I meant stars like the ones on TV
before I knew you I was nobody

when you type the word *stars* into Google Brad Pitt's and
Dale Winton's faces appear on the screen
before they were stars they were... I meant the ones in the
sky
stars

not all the cloud of dust ends up as part of a star
some of the remaining dust can become planets or asteroids
or comets
or some of it just remains as dust like the stuff on your shelf
some stars become Brad Pitt

before they were stars they were dust

Famous Billys

Billy Blake	Billy Shakespeare	Billy Wordsworth
Bill I Am	Billy Tell	Billy Wallace
Billy the Conqueror	Billy Shatner	Billy Wilberforce
Prince Billy	Venus Billys	Serena Billys
Robin Billys	Hank Billys	

You are a fake Facebook post / A photograph taken on Westminster Bridge during a terrorist attack / The face of a woman walking calmly past as if she didn't care / Posted by a Russian troll / The conversation turns like the museum notes at the side of a painting / The ones you read before you even look at the work / Telling you what to think / Clichés that offer no insight / Let your eyes do the feeling and your heart do the thinking / Your eyes are Leonardo da Vinci's greatest hits / Your memory is Queen's *Greatest Hits* 1 and 2 / The lines on your face are a Basquiat painting / And they're selling postcards of your face in the museum shop / All new and not scratched-up yet / Your minor arguments are like buying a new pair of white trainers / The first time you kick a football you can hear the shiny leather scream / Your attitude is a remote-control sucker punch / You know what combination of buttons to press to get a reaction / Your life protected like a Perspex-covered Banksy on the wall of a London street / People only like it cos it's a Banksy / And it's expensive / And simplistic / You laugh like a V-formation of geese flying overhead / You can hear the beat of the wing / And it's beautiful / And I die laughing with you.

I Am Related To Every Single Human Being On The Planet*

** I really like the scientific theory/fact that everyone can trace their family tree back to one woman, a Mitochondrial Eve, who lived in East Africa 200,000 years ago, a maternal ancestor to all living humans with an unbroken lineage, making her the mother of the whole human race. I wonder if she had any idea that she would become the great-great-great-great-great recurring grandmother to the Queen, to the President of the United States, to the rich, to the poor, to mothers and to murderers, to everyone, and to me. If she could see me now I hope she would not be disappointed.*

we are really hard on each other
considering we are so imperfect
but these imperfections are what make us beautiful
there is nothing wrong with you
you are beautiful

like an unfinished painting
that looks like it has been painted by a five-year-old
but when you try to do it yourself
you realise it takes years of practice
to learn how not to draw
you have paved over your skill
made a patio of yourself
have you ever tried to make a mark or line like a five-year-old?
I have and it's almost impossible

we delude ourselves and appear foolishly sophisticated

we need to find the brushstrokes in the words

there is nothing worse than a soulless shiny brand-new straight-
edged building
no cracks to peer into to see beneath the surface
where all the dust and drama is

the same as people
I only trust people with cracks and dust and drama

if I ever do anything of any real importance
I will be disappointed
because I know I will be doing it wrong
and impressing all the wrong people

They Never Met Their Match

Simon and Ant
Ant and Cannon
Cannon and French
French and Laurel
Laurel and Morecambe
Morecambe and Thelma
Thelma and Romeo
Romeo and Bonnie
Bonnie and Pinky
Pinky and Butch
Butch and Yin
Yin and Tom
Tom and Torvill
Torvill and Adam
Adam and Thompson
Thompson and Tweedledum
The One Ronnie
Jackson One
Fun Boy One
The One Degree
The Marx Brother
The Fab One
The One Top
Dave Clarke
Secret One
Famous One
Fantastic One

One Samurai
The 1st Sense
One Mile
One Man and a Baby
One Musketeer
The Magnificent One
One Thing I Hate About You
One Day Later
One Dalmatian
Ocean's One
Hawaii One-O
One Angry Man

I Stole The Sky

I think dreams are really all nightmares / Like the time I stole the sky / No one had the sky to look up to / The sun had no place to shine / The rain had no place to fall from / The clouds had no place to float / And the stars had no place to sparkle or shoot / The responsibility of owning the sky exhausted me / I knew everyone would be angry and upset if they knew I had stolen the sky / I hid it in my cupboard / Buried it under some old clothes and tried to forget about it / I've also seen pink spaceships stealing the sun and the shadows / Like I said at the beginning / All dreams are nightmares really.

Boredom is...

a)   a multiple-choice poem ☐

b)   a gluten-free bakery with no customers and
        overpriced weak coffee ☐

c)   a Facebook feed with no comments and no likes ☐

d)   a scorched lawn during the summer of 2018 ☐

e)   a poem that is really an advert that is selling
        something that none of us can afford to lose ☐

f)   none of the above ☐

g)   all of the above ☐

I grew up along the banks of the Thames
Its face looked like John Wayne
I haven't seen a John Wayne film or the Thames for a long time
I wonder if they still look the same

the house looks like Bill Murray in *Lost in Translation*
and everyday looks like Bill Murray in *Groundhog Day*
and Sunday with the kids looks like Bill Murray in *Ghostbusters*

but the whole world looks like Jack Nicholson in *As Good as
It Gets*

Carl Andre's Bricks

Carl Andre / Exhausted from a day's labouring / Ends his twelve-hour shift at the Wimpey building site / An incomplete, uninspiring brand new estate of mediocre family homes / He slumps into his clapped-out, rusted Ford Fiesta / Whilst his mind stews and boils over the gardening and DIY he needs to finish at home / So he doesn't get an earful of abuse from his missus.

As he approaches the entrance to the site / The security team is nowhere to be seen / So there is no one to lift the barrier for Carl to leave / He stops the car / Pulls up the handbrake / Keeps the juddering engine running / Sluggishly gets out and walks over to the barrier / It is here he notices a crate of new bricks that haven't been taken safely onto the site yet / He could use those bricks to finish the garden wall that would then be lined with roses and an assortment of other flowers / He would be in his wife's good books for once if he finally managed to finish some of the jobs he had started / He quickly grabs five or six bricks at a time / And begins to load them into the boot of his car / One hundred and twenty bricks loaded without anyone noticing / His car suspension drooping / The bumper brushing any raised tarmac.

He arrives home safely and unpacks the stolen load in a systematic and precise manner onto the front lawn / Two layers of sixty bricks arranged six bricks in width by ten bricks in length / Looking down at his ready-made sculpture he ponders to himself / *That looks good enough to be hung in the Tate* / His thought pattern is disrupted by his wife who is yelling from the second-floor open window / "Carl Andre, why are you home late again? / You been down the pub? / My mother told me not to marry a no-goodun like you!" / Carl drops his chin and trudges off to the garage to collect his tools to start building the garden wall.

Lowry put down his paintbrush after painting some more matchstick men and matchstick cats and dogs / It was Sunday and he was trying to figure out what he was doing in life / The anguish on people's faces was etched into his fingers / Off-white pigment trapped under his yellowing nails / Reminding him of his solitude.

Even at dinner / After he had scrubbed his hands / The pigment dug dirt deep under his skin / Recalling to his mind every man's loneliness / Every pea / Carrot / Slice of potato he swallowed became caught in his throat / Like he was choking on sorrow.

True Art Truant

Picasso stood at the school gates
looking hard at how narrow the corridors were
how sealed shut the doors
how chiselled the children
how grey and glazed their eyes
no art today
imagination has been taken away
I think I'll stay at home in my head

They sat in the long grass / Between the bus stop and the
hospital / Right where the rats would run / They looked like
a romantic impressionist painting on the verge of the Whipps
Cross roundabout.

There is always an ice-cream van outside the Tate making
lining up for a 99 a work of art

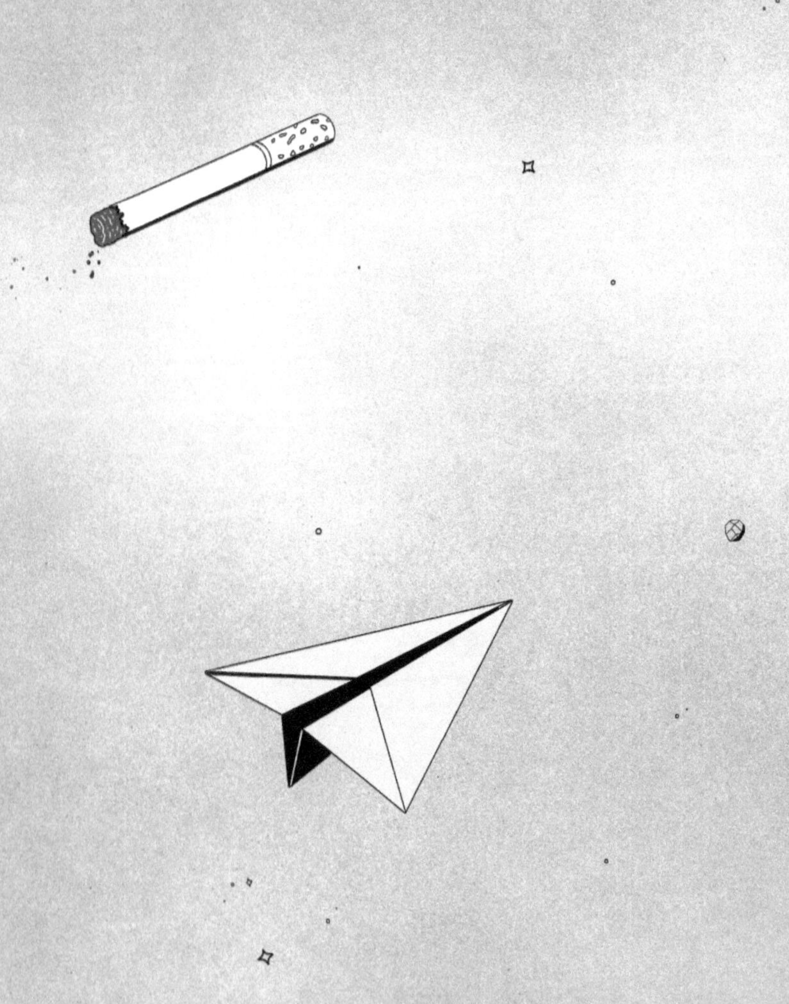

Jupiter

I found a shell that looked like the wing of a butterfly
and when I held it to my ear it was as silent as a wing beat

A Wish For The Lonely And The Young

One in four of you will harm yourselves / One in four of you will suffer from depression / Thousands of you each year will dance from a bridge / They will try to fix you rather than fix the world they have created around you / The real world can give you everything you desire / The invented world will destroy you and make you feel you don't exist / You are plenty and powerful and enough and all you ever need / And I wish / You would study the crest of waves / You would walk the beaches picking up fossils as you go / Reminding you how old the universe is / And how young you are / I wish you would drink milkshake with your friends / And talk about poetry / And what it was like the first time you heard a sentence that made you feel you were being rolled out like Plasticine / I wish you would dive under the sea to meet octopus / And understand that they are as intelligent as you but see the world differently / I wish it was compulsory to study daydreams in school / To help you realise daydreams are real / And to know that social media isn't real / And that living in the digital age teaches you more about loneliness than technology.

Hate is a Facebook thread / A frenzy of blame / With people tying themselves in lassoed knots / With tumbleweed thoughts / And a rotting teeth old-timer of ideas / Choking themselves with their own whip / And a blade to their own throat / Like a revenge movie / Mounting horses led by a bitter drunken deputy / The self-appointed judge and jury / Chasing down the accused / Like a Wild West vigilante mob / In a small dust-windblown lawless town.

You can hear their brains rattling / Like battered tins on the back of a slow-moving mule / Making its way upstream to pan for gold / And their minds pose at windows like prostitutes / Their cleavage pushed up in corsets with protruding breasts / Wanting likes and responses / Like the wink or the mean glare of an unshaven stranger in a Stetson / While inserting a laughing-whilst-crying emoji.

If the mob don't get ya the rattlesnakes will / Or the heat of the sun as you lift the watering can to your mouth / And empty the last drop of humanity onto your tongue / The shit flows freely down the street because there is no filter or sewage system / Just a hole in the ground overflowing with piss / And cheap shots / And stupidity.

How easily they get us to turn on each other like dogs in a pit / Whilst vultures circle our thoughts / Waiting for ideas to die / So they can rip and claw the eyes and heart out of them.

I stole the line 'Frenzy of Blame' from the title of a Robert Pollard song, similar to the way a cowboy would steal a stallion in the Wild West.

you fold like a paper aeroplane
when thrown from the top window you fly
and float on the breeze with such ease

but you land on the wet grass
the dew soaks into your creases
the fall buckles your pointed nose
rips your carefully turned corners

and you can fly no more

We spent the night kissing in crash helmets to protect ourselves from a fall / But every time our lips touched we bumped our heads / Our visors would steam up and push against our soft skin / Creating marks and bruises after every peck / We thought it would be safe but we were wrong / Kissing in crash helmets is no fun.

Dave buried his head in the sand / But how did he do it? / He thought it was going to be easy / But his first attempts were a failure / Digging the hole was easy enough / But filling in the hole with his head lowered beneath the surface of the earth proved exceedingly difficult / Having to reach around and push the dirt and sand back over his head was an impossible task / Every time he reached forward to shovel the sand into the hole / His head would lift from its lowered position / And force more sand out the hole / It became obvious after several attempts he needed assistance if he was to successfully bury his head in the sand / But finding someone to do the job was also very difficult / Everyone he asked just pointed out the obvious / "You're just burying your head in the sand Dave" / "But can you help me do it?" he asked / "No, you need to face up and confront your problems Dave / It's the only way / I know it's difficult but you'll thank me later" / So Dave metaphorically buried his head in the sand / Whilst he thought about how he was actually going to bury his head in the sand / Whilst all his friends and colleagues talked and whispered behind his back about how he was just burying his head in the sand.

If people were retail goods, you'd probably take them back to the shop and say, "There's something wrong with this one. Can I get a refund, please?"

"Would you like another one?" the shop assistant would ask.

"No, thank you, it's faulty, it doesn't do what I want it to do, I just want to get my money back!"

Some people would take themselves back to the shop to get a refund.

Freedom is...

a)   a low credit score when trying to get a
      mortgage   ☐

b)   a hacked computer with all your personal
      details on file which can be shared with
      everyone at anytime but nobody cares   ☐

c)   a bank robber that never gets caught   ☐

d)   none of the above   ☐

e)   all of the above   ☐

Don't Push In

He puts it like this.

"It's like being in a restaurant line / And we were here first / You don't want others to push into the line, do you?"

But we are not in the line / We are already in the restaurant / Eating and drinking / But the food in the restaurant is unpalatable / Not because of the food / But because of the company / Because of people like him.

And I try to convince him that there are enough seats and tables / And there is plenty of room to put out more seats and tables / There doesn't need to be a line.

But he'll never be convinced / He tells them to get to the back of the line / To wait their turn / To go back to their own restaurant / To their own line / To go back to their own country.

Can I get the bill, please? / Keep the change.

the farm that grew humanity
suffered five years of heavy drought
creating a dust bowl of hate

the butterfly lifted the elephant from the ground
and the silver-foil swans flew away from the table

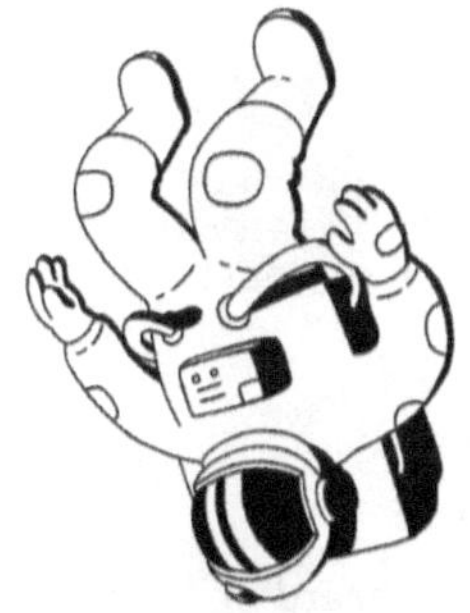

What We Lost In The Fire
(Written one year before a tower block burns)

Warm the coffee in plastic cups
Heat the base with lighted match
Concrete over the sky
Plaster over the cracks
Cover the creaking
Crackling sun

Sell the ceiling to the highest bidder
Microwave the sea
Exchange cash for a peerage
Buy your first-class degree
Bomb a town we've never heard of
Become a Nobel Peace Prize nominee
Bestow awards for outstanding services to the environment
Chop down the last tree
Pull the wings off the last bee
Burn the last bit of toast
And smother it in honey

Burn a whole generation
To a white-hot cinder
Chuck 'em on the charcoal pit
So they will burn longer
Along with their kids
And their kids
And their kids

Why care?
Don't stop there!

Keep throwing fuel on the fire
The good-for-nothing guzzling gutless gaslight glow
Will keep you warm at night
Do not piss on them
Do not extinguish the flame
We wouldn't want dreams to be ignited now would we?

Have you heard the one about this generation having terrible
punctuation question mark?
They can't tell a full stop from a forced stop
A comma from a deep coma
A colon from the large intestine that extends from their
rectum
An apostrophe from an apostle
But it's not the teaching that's bad
The teachers are not to blame
This generation can't even breathe
They're fighting for air
So when would they have time to practice reading riting
rithmetic?

The trick
Collapse culture like a box

Lock education in a lab as if it is a disease
That needs to be studied
Controlled
Vaccinate the precious privileged few
Let their drivel dribble
Their sick ideas
Swarm and multiply
Like bacteria in a rotting brain

Put out the candle
Ignite the kindle
Refuse to cuddle
Deny love ever existed

So they can't see love
Can't see the flames through the fire
I can't see love
Watch their faces melt
Watch their lives melt

See me
Six out of ten
Could have done better
Hell for leather
Hands for leather
Soft leather hands
Hard leather heart
Feel the back of my leather hand
Feel the back of my leather heart

My worn-out leather heart
Full of holes
I made the holes
I punched them there
So I could pull my belt tighter
Pull it tighter
What's the matter?
Can't breathe
Buckle up boys
Buckle up
Tighten your belts
Tighten your brains
Tighten your dreams

Burn a generation
Because we lost our hopes and minds in the fire

We wouldn't want other people's dreams to be ignited now
would we?

I was on the Tube
hundreds of people got on at London Bridge
and I knew every single one of them

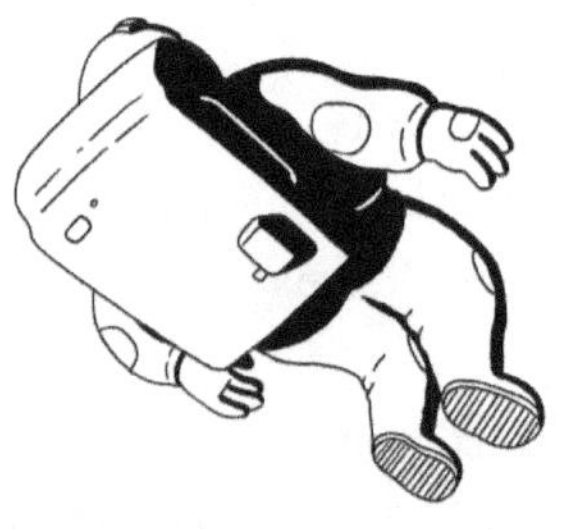

this is the Bacteria line
this train is ready to leave
please stand clear of the closing doors

her nails match the chipped red handrail of the
underground train
the ripped advertising posters
an unconscious and energised aesthetic

Splitting Atoms

on the train
between London and Newcastle
two young mathematicians discuss
quantum mechanics, X and Why?

they both come to the same conclusion

when he leaves the carriage
she waves goodbye
they go their separate ways
the apple drops
and he wishes
they could
go back in time

On the down escalator / Your hazel eyes act like gravity / And it makes me ask questions / Like is the sun lonely? / The answers come hurtling towards me / Like burning meteors / Earthbound.

The scene looks like one of those selfie smartphone apps / That make stars and hearts come out your eyes when you blink / And rainbow rays of light zoom out your mouth when we kiss.

A week later it made me feel lonely / Like a man with a selfie stick in front of the Leaning Tower of Pisa / With no one to take his photograph.

I am not sure you are even human / More like a robot who is learning to be alive / And when we meet / It feels like a scene from an early 1970s sci-fi TV drama / Where I wonder if it is possible to fall in love with a machine / The same way people fall in love with their cars or their phones.

And you speak about your father and his military history / And how you are tired of trying to live up to his perfect vision for you / And I imagine how he and his team created your beauty in a top-secret military lab / To use you in special undercover missions / But when it came to it / It was just too dangerous / That you might be found out / And they wouldn't want this technology falling into enemy hands.

Anyway / Your father fell deeply in love with his creation / As if you were his very own daughter / And he taught you to live / But

kept you at a safe distance from the world / Until now / Where
you drink two bottles of wine with a poet / Whilst the couples
at other tables / Fall in love with their phones and their cars.

Extinct

I love you like a million dinosaurs after the meteorite hit
wiping them from the Earth
the impact causing an explosion in my heart
two million times greater than a nuclear bomb

birds and crocodiles still exist so I suppose romance isn't dead

the bright young palaeontologist
breaking sedimentary rocks open all day with a rock hammer
finding fossils but never finding love

it's all about timing
finding things millions of years old
but never being able to break yourself open
to reveal your inner fossil
to find something as fresh and as instant and as ancient as love

she was a bullet in the head
an ice-cream ghost

she was a dimmed light after closing time
the blue buzz of an electric fly zapper
breathing ultraviolet instead of oxygen

she was your very own horror story

the body of your brother
on a coroner's cold slab
a whiplash slapdash busted face mugshot
cheeks mangled
teeth shattered

because ghosts haunt your head not your house

she was the magic of rainfall and sunrise
the blossom in her eyes
the wing beat of a butterfly
on a silent Scotch-soaked pastel-lip-kissed breeze

it can take you by surprise
how fleeting the fragile flicker fades into the distance

opening the car door
riding the bus
stroking a crazed dog
a toke on a shared cigarette
a slug of whisky
a tragic benevolent violence

the cars behind beep me
as I look for rainbows at the red light
the coffee connects me to a morning reality
a dog barks at ghosts

London peers in through a bug-splattered windscreen
saves money by cutting people's throats
burning people's coats
discovering black sludge to heat second homes

skin full of bone
bone in my sawdust head
listen to one lie two lie
three lie in my bed

words creep from me
rather than hurtle like a crazy rain-soaked waterfall
the cars behind beep me
as I look for rainbows at the red light

Space Junk

Space is a dark sky full of clouds of debris / That float above our big ball of dirt / Half a million objects left over from a spaceman's all-inclusive holiday to the moon / Or a joyride of burnt-out broken-down satellites abandoned on the hard shoulder of Earth's atmosphere / We've littered space like a bank holiday festival in the sky / Treat it like a teenage bedroom / With a KEEP OUT toxic skull and crossbones sign hung on the door / That hasn't seen sunlight for months / And no parent dares to enter fearful of what they might find lurking on the carpet or under the bedsheets / Who is cleaning up this mess? / Can I suggest using a space bin?

Anxiety is...

a)   an old man with an irrational fear of birds
        feeding pigeons in Trafalgar Square in the
        1970s   ☐

b)   a milkshake with no milk and no shake   ☐

c)   a shoe with a hole in its soul   ☐

d)   a heart attack on the motorway at the wheel
        of a heavy goods vehicle   ☐

e)   all of the above   ☐

f)   none of the above   ☐

Tomorrow's Fish And Chip Wrapping

she wrapped my fat chips in yesterday's news
except the news wasn't made of paper
it was a laptop screen and an old iPhone
and the vinegar went everywhere

Eye Glass / Glass Eye

my reading glasses stop me looking into the distance
or what I see in the distance is blurry
like they're trying to stop me from reading my own future

Neanderthal man is at the campsite / Everyone else has brought matches to light their camping stoves / He has brought flint and some kindling / His tent is made of willow / He doesn't wash up / Doesn't need to / He eats his food with his hands / And off a leaf when necessary / A few people's dogs have gone missing / But Neanderthal man's barbecues are second to none / The shower thing he finds hilarious / Camping is easy when you know how.

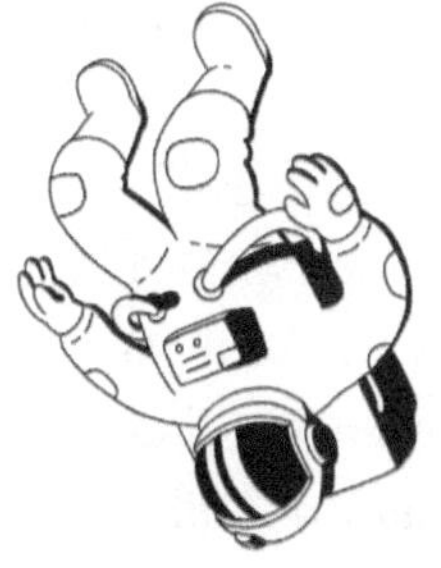

My grandad was one of the quietest people I knew / When the family were in a rage and having heated discussions about someone or something / My grandad would listen but say nothing / He'd just stand with a pint of homebrew in the corner / And listen to it all kicking off.

Everyone else with their elevated sense of opinion / He'd just let them get it off their chest / Once he surprised everyone by saying to my mum / "But it might not be like that Pat" / But my mum shouted him down and kept ranting / And I looked on and thought / *Yeah, he's right, it might not be like that.*

I'd find him in the garden / Growing vegetables and flowers / He became a real self-taught expert / He took over four of the neighbours' gardens / And kept them stocked up with potatoes / Carrots / Tomatoes / Onions / Red and green peppers / Sweetcorn / Runner beans / Beetroot / Parsnips / And a whole array of other veg throughout the year.

All his family had died by the time he was nineteen / His mum / Dad / Brother / And sisters all gone / He sat alone in a terraced house wondering what he should do / So he joined the army for company / When I asked him about the war or the army he always said the same thing / "I peeled potatoes."

Up until the day he died I always believed he just peeled potatoes / Didn't occur to me he just didn't want to talk about it / If I asked / He'd give me the usual answer / And then take me into his garden to look at the flowers / Or birds / Or just the beauty of it all.

If he had something important to say then he'd say it / But he made me realise / That *it might not be like that* / And a potato peeler might not just be a potato peeler.

Wisdom is...

a)   a half-eaten KFC bargain bucket ☐

b)   a long putt on the 18th hole in a downpour ☐

c)   a quiet conversation with your other self ☐

d)   all of the above ☐

e)   none of the above ☐

My grandad was an armchair pirate / Captain James Hook was his name / A hook for a hand / Used to tap the TV remote control with the tip to turn on the snooker / A patch for an eye / Kept his hearing aid in his snuffbox / His teeth in a jewelled goblet next to his bed / He was a keen gardener / After he died I found a treasure map on his bedside table / With a large X marking the spot / But I couldn't bring myself to dig up his prize-winning roses.

I lost my sense of humour
down the back of the sofa
all I found in its place
was fake laughter

TV adverts grate my nerves more than usual / I crave culture / I hear lorries sing like a Welsh choir as they trundle past / We're madder than ever / All on the edge of cliffs / With only a wedding as a reprieve to make us feel normal / And who feels normal at a wedding? / No one / I'm sure the WiFi is in our heads making us feel sick / Everyone I talk to is ill or sick or mad / Maybe it's our age / Maybe I was right all along / Maybe I'm old and mad / The motorbikes move along the road like a dragon coughing.

A Poem About Daytime TV

flick
flick
shit
shit
flick
shit
flick flick
shit
flick flick
shit shit
flick
flick
shit
flick
shit
shit
flick shit
shit
shit
shit
flick
shit
flick flick
shit flick
flick
shit shit
flick
flick

off

Insurmountable Tasks

getting out of bed
answering the phone
making a call
filling in a form
looking you in the eye
looking anyone in the eye
talking
talking to anyone
breathing
breathing
breathe

my flower is a windmill
it might blow away
and it will be a nothing flower

oh dear
a moth has just flown in
he'll spend his time trying to have sex with the LED light
and almost burning himself to death
thinking it's the moon or something

and I'll just sit here watching
feeling sorry for him

the butterfly lifted the Earth

balanced it gently on its tongue

and slowly spun it with the repeated beat of a patterned wing

when I hold my phone in the air to capture a moment
I see loneliness screaming at me

so far it's all been a big mistake

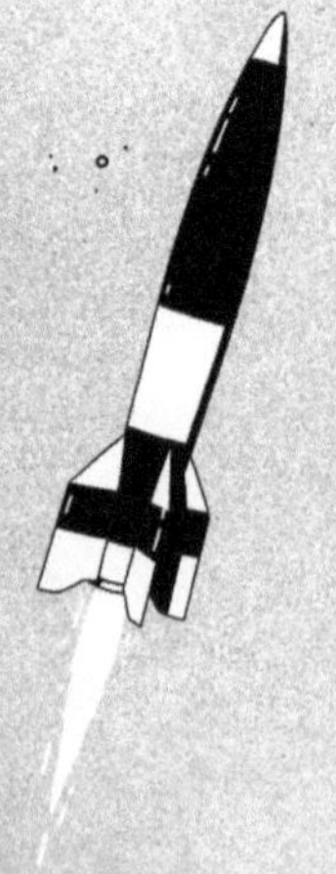

Saturn

even when I'm offered the whole chair I sit on the edge

Spoken word makes me want to fly passenger planes into tall towers filled with burning people / The way you talk and act is like a terrorist attack on my senses / My eyes and ears are Westminster Bridge / Your words a speeding car / And when you open your mouth and drive at me with speed / I want to jump off and drown in the river below.

Imagine when you spoke your voice played music instead of speaking words / And when you said something out loud / People would dance to the sound of your voice.

When you told someone you loved them / Your voice would play 'Suzanne' by Leonard Cohen / And they would fall in love with you / As you touched their perfect body with your mind.

And when you were angry / You would bellow out some angry drum 'n' bass / And the person who your anger was directed at / Would feel overcome with energy and ecstasy / And dance dance dance right in front of you / And inside feel exactly what you meant.

And they wouldn't get confused about the message / Unlike talking / As you stumble and tumble over your words / They would just feel the rhythm and the sound and understand completely.

And when you phone up customer services / And they put you on hold / You'd shout down the phone / "Don't put me on hold!" / And elevator music would be sent down the phone / Drowning out their own ambient crackle.

Whilst out for dinner / Your date would ask you to order the wine / And you'd sing the sweetest tune to the waiter / And be served the best wine in their cellar / Or if they disliked the song / A carafe of cheap house white.

And the people would get you to speak at political rallies / And your music would make all the politicians stop and listen / To listen harder than they have ever listened before / And they would dance and move freely to the agony and unjustness / To the hurt and unfairness of it all / And make real social change / Whilst dancing to the music that you spoke.

I see inside a lot of poets
I see an academic heart
an intellectual heart
a theatrical heart
a political heart
a storytelling heart
but most of the time I don't see a poetry heart
they are not really poets
they are something else in waiting
disguised as a poet

Criminal Eyes

capital eyes
capital lies
capitalise

radical eyes
radical lies
radicalise

idol eyes
idol lies
idolise

marginal eyes
marginal lies
marginalise

immortal eyes
immortal lies
immortalise

natural eyes
natural lies
naturalise

actual eyes
actual lies
actualise

legal eyes
legal lies
legalise

How Do Bats Navigate?

It is a little-known fact / That the bat uses high-frequency poetry to navigate / Poetry that the human ear cannot hear / Minute poetry waves bouncing off small things that have a big meaning / Using echolocation to find truth and dinner / Things that lie and fly undetected to the human eye.

Ultrasound poetry does not travel far / So humans are not in tune to receive the words of the bard bat beat / Speed-of-sound poetry / Words vibrating at 340 metres per second / Makes grime sound like a gentle stroll in the park on a Sunday morning.

Unlike elephant poetry which is very low and can travel over long distances / We have all seen and heard the elephant poets stomping all over the undergrowth / Next time / Try and listen out for the poetry of the bat / They can help us navigate the world.

Vomit

vandal eyes
vandal lies
vandalise

odour eyes
odour lies
odourise

material eyes
material lies
materialise

irrational eyes
irrational lies
irrationalise

traditional eyes
traditional lies
traditionalise

you write like you want to be loved by the same people who appear on *Gogglebox* and the same people who get a kick out of watching *X Factor*

you write like you're trying to impress Simon Cowell
all tight T-shirts and fake tans
and jeans pulled up and belted above your waist

Emptiness is...

*tick correct box

a) an author typing as if he was performing a piano concerto to a dying star ☐

b) human bombs full of love falling on a village ☐

c) a grey ghost in a grey fog standing next to a grey house ☐

d) a wasp attempting to land safely in a pint of beer without drowning ☐

e) a poet going to the Queen's house for tea ☐

f) none of the above ☐

g) all of the above ☐

I feel the same as Ivor Cutler did
the time I saw him reading his poems
and a mobile phone interrupted his set
and he looked up from his tiny book and said
"I hate this world."

I sit in the garden writing poems in my top hat
birds gather round and listen to my mind whirr

What Did I Steal To Write This Poem?

I stole a language
I stole ideas
I stole words written by other poets
I stole a kiss
I stole moments that were only meant for you

I'm writing
like a tangled rose bush
thorny and in bloom
the kids are playing hide-and-seek in small rooms
with nowhere to hide except behind the door
count to ten
here I come
ready or not
found you

Not A Real Writer

I am a writer
I forgot my pen
the only pen I had on me was my EpiPen
so I stabbed myself in the leg
and wrote this poem

Real Writers Use Bic Pens

anyone who uses a different pen is a faker
I wrote this on my iPhone

She was the universe / When she stared up at the night sky /
It was like she was looking at herself in an invisible mirror /
Seeing inside herself / Revealing secrets only the universe could
know / Stories passed down over the aeons / Held faintly in the
dim light of distant stars for her to read.

I will hang out on a Californian beach selling ice cream / And with every ice cream sold the person will get a free book of poetry and a pocket calculator / I will ask them to read the book and then make comments only using the pocket calculator / The only word they will be able to spell with the calculator will be BOOBS (80085) / And so BOOBS will be the results of my research.

I will jet off to the moon where I will shout questions to the world that no one can hear / The world will shout back with answers that I cannot hear / And I will write them down with my pointing finger in moon dust / These words will only be disturbed when an astronaut steps on them with a moon boot.

just walked through a tunnel
and this poem was blown out of me

little ruins

sketches

not real poems

effervescent lines that bubble to the surface and break

do words know when it is time to go to bed?

I want to retire with my binoculars to my garden / To look at the birds feeding on the bird feeder / Admire their work / Their grace and their magic / In awe of their ballet and their song.

It's hard for other people to take / When you tell them all you want to do is write poetry / "But you can't pay the bills writing poetry!" / I know / But it can do / "Writing poetry won't feed your kids!" / I know / But it might do / So much good advice / They never really tell you what will pay the bills / Sometimes they say work hard and hard work / I work hard at writing poetry / It pays.

The only job he ever wanted growing up was to be Father Christmas / He wanted to be the real thing / So in preparation / When he was old enough / He grew a long beard / Put on a few pounds / And made a classic red Father Christmas suit.

Unfortunately / After waiting many years for his beard to turn a pure white / Father Christmas no longer existed.

I've been wearing a 'Baby On Board' badge on the lapel of
my coat
I'm not pregnant
I just like badges
and sitting down when travelling

it's next to my anarchist badge
I'm not an anarchist
but I think you'll agree
that wearing an anarchist badge
and not being an anarchist
is quite a strong statement

I saw it glistening in the sun / Like a huge spaceship on its side / Sparkling in the light / It was waiting for us / All of us / Yet no one knew what to do.

come to me
effortlessly
like a bomb

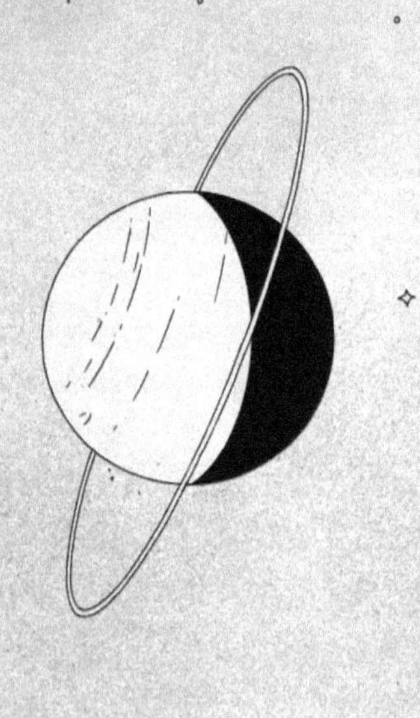

Uranus

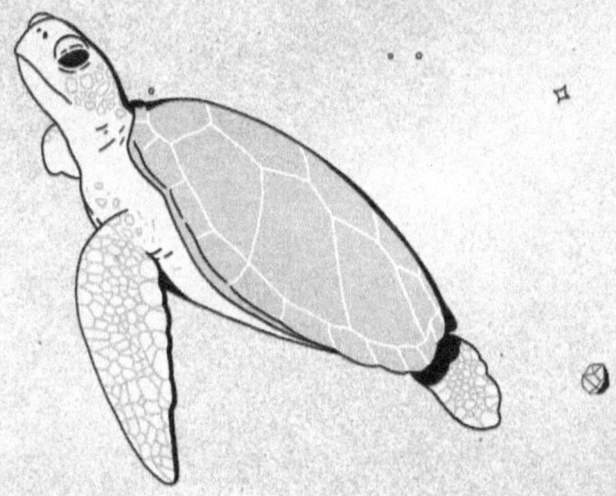

even the light is sad here
sunbeams are made out of tears

my blood
made of liquid mercury
reaches my fingertips

my brain
a dusty cupboard under the stairs
shudders at the thought of sunlight

when I think of everyone I love
or have ever loved
I cry

tension trapped inside a diving bell

today the clouds look amazing and ordinary at the same time
maybe it's my eyes that are amazing

your eyes are amazing
baptised in sunbeam blue

I cry in my sleep
you cry in my head
we cry in my heart
sometimes we even cry tears
wade depths with giant turtles
where the moon contains our fears

my face
a rain cloud
sad all the time
even when laughing

I sit
look around at all the different faces
I can't help feel the human race failed

we didn't want to survive

living makes you hard
it plunders daydreams
I don't want my kids to grow up hard
I want their daydreams to be real

Old Friends Are Just A Memory Of When You Last Met

when I saw you in the supermarket
you looked like you'd been hit by a car
but you hadn't
you'd been drinking

if only we could stay as kids
scrambling in the forest
away from the grown-ups
and laugh like that
and love like that
and hurt like that
so painful
so extreme
so alive

share our ideas
stupid ones
genius ones
and let them all slide
into oblivion
without a care

just lie back on the grass
looking at the sky
wondering
when will this end

and when it ends
you run so fast
round so many corners
and over so many hurdles
that you can't find your way back there
to that magical place

it's as if it didn't exist at all

and when you lose all hope of finding your way home
you drink yourself to death

Pebble

to build castles in sand
only to be knocked down by the tide
wall of grain by wall of grain

to miss my friend as much
as he misses the sun
in the arctic winter

to splinter my thoughts with sorrow

to not know the place
or the back of my hand
to miss my friend
the fading castle
the sand

your mind is like a bleached coral reef
a change of temperature of one or two degrees causes
devastation
but we'll treat it like thunder
we'll pretend it's the clouds bashing together
Earth seen from a spaceship is like an atomic bomb
mushroom cloud
it looks beautiful from a distance
but close up
when you're in it
it's like burning ants with a magnifying glass
focusing the sun's rays on their armoured backs
and setting them on fire

when sadness cuts through you like a bullet train with no
brakes
you think about your friends
what they really are
who they really are
the insides of them
their internal workings
what they feel
their eyes

they do not see you struggle to hang onto the cliff face of hope
with your fingernails digging deep into the cliff edge of life
your feet dangling in a computer-generated death

pull me up
please

instead you choose to tread on my fingertips like a villain from
the silver screen

I will go to the cinema by myself and there will be no one else in the cinema when the film is playing and the room will be dark much darker than my mind and the film is bad and the darkness makes me feel alone and the absence of people makes me feel lonely and wish I wasn't sitting in a large dark room watching a bad film that no one else is watching when outside there are crowds of people and the sun is shining but I stay and watch the whole film till the end and spend two hours thinking about how lonely I am.

Happy and Sad sat next to each other on a park bench
not touching
not looking at each other
hardly even breathing

"did you see the sky last night?" asked Happy

"yeah, did you?"

"yeah, me too"

"how did it make you feel" asked Sad

"it made me feel happy"

"oh, it made me feel sad" said Sad

"strange, same sky."

she swallowed the sun
and the beams shone out from her
but others now lived in darkness

so she was forced to climb high into the sky
and let her light shine down on others
so they could see

but the responsibility was too much
and she burnt out
and sank beneath the horizon

and sadness rose from her eyes like the dawn
knowing she had to do it again and again
as if no one cared

on this road
everything is a traffic light
laughter seems so far from here
and it's getting dark

I wanted to ride dragonflies
skim across the water and reeds on their golden backs
but that thought disappeared
when the men came
and stole the smiles
and replaced them with nothing worth knowing

apart from this road where everything is a traffic light
and it's getting dark

is it dark yet?
yeah, it's really dark

I polished my shoes with spit and sadness
brushed them to a brilliant shine
so I could see my own reflection in the black gloss
when the sunlight caught the toe

de press

deep press

deep rest

deep press shone

the opposite of loneliness
a rainforest, a coral reef, the stars
knowing you are the universe
falling and fighting a bear
sinking into soft grass and looking up at the sky
whispering
"I know you, I know you, I know who you are."

The Most Beautiful Man In The World

he is the most
beautiful
man in the
world

when he laughs
I am happy
for him
when he sleeps
I am happy
for him
when he hugs
his mum and dad
I am happy
for them

a stranger
may not see that
he is the most
beautiful
man in the
world

to us
the world is
confusing
but to him

it is like
clouds
on a clear day
or blue sky
when it should be
grey

his mum sits
on the sofa
crying
she is tired
because her son is
alone
not from lack of
love
but because his
burden
is to be
alone

to be the most
beautiful
man in the
world
you must be
alone

his brother Victor
loves him
his brother cares
for him
when he cries
Victor says
Mum
Dad
Stanley is
crying
he cares for his
brother
he loves him
dearly

to suffer this
a punishment
the rewards must be
great
a reward
unseen

the boy
on his dad's back
is the most
beautiful
boy in the
world

sometimes you feel
that you want
to get
hold of him
to squeeze him
to squeeze him
so tight
that you might
squeeze out
of him his
condition

but this may also
squeeze out his
beauty

for he is the most
beautiful
man in the
world

Loneliness is a playground full of children / With no one to play with / Ten aeroplanes in the sky with jet trails / And Gary tying a knot round his neck / Hanging himself from the monkey-bar ropes / His body being held up by the dinner ladies by his legs / Trying desperately to push him up / So he wouldn't strangle himself to death.

I cling to you like a wheezing breath

Loneliness is...

a)   a common sadness ☐

b)   a wild horse on a rain-soaked windy moor ☐

c)   a sharp metal spade digging the dirt of your insides ☐

d)   a mad scientist's laboratory whose inventions set fire to themselves ☐

e)   a little green man with his head popping out of a moon crater ☐

f)   none of the above ☐

g)   all of the above ☐

The slot-machine winnings / The rattle and clatter of coins falling like tears into metal troughs / The arcades and amusement parks are the loneliest places in the world / The bumper cars bumping each other / Again and again like smashing heads / Swirling around and around and around in the same direction forever / The motion sickness of the spinning wheels / The feeling of waking every morning alone / Knowing you have to feed the machine / And it will take everything you have ever earned.

An Attempt At Remedy

If your loneliness is a very large hole you cannot fill / I will come and empty all my kids' toys into it / I will tip all the paintings and all the films I have ever seen into the void / All the conversations I've ever had / I will push in every scene from every time I stopped the car to survey the landscape / I will dump all the weapons of the world into the chasm / The warships / The planes / The tanks / The missiles / The guns / The bullets / Every last one of them / And I will shovel in all the moments where I did not need to speak and silence made the room complete / And after all this / I hope there will be no space left to fill.

Mural

I've spent a lot of time
painting over my life
in thick paint
reworking and reimagining how my life should be

if I look back to how my life used to be
I can no longer see it
it is covered in a blanket of colour
a very unremarkable fresco

even if I chipped away the layers
it wouldn't be there
all mixed up and blended
with magnolias and soft apple hues

the heavy builders would need to be brought in to remove it
all hammer and chisels

no archaeologist
would want to take the time or care
to preserve it
or to X-ray the spot
to see beneath the surface

but if they did
in a moment of misguided curiosity
they'd only see
an un-extraordinary sadness
the stuff you see painted over
on every mundane street and face

Retail Therapy

there should be a shop
where you can rent
a smile for a while
or a long weekend

there should be a place
where you can go
to buy a laugh
for a close friend

the receipt's in the bag
so you can take it back
if it's the wrong one
or if it doesn't fit

is there an
out-of-town megastore
with giggles for sale
stacked high on shelves?

buy two chuckles
get one free
a scream of joy
with same-day delivery

a Laughter World
to upgrade your snigger
to make it much bigger

with 50% off
an ear-to-ear grin

titters for under a tenner
off the peg
or made to measure

a chortle on mail order
because sadness always seems to be
just around the corner

I'm Not Sure How Many Planets There Are In The Solar System Anymore

Too much wine presses heavy on a watermark memory / You blank them / Black them out / But when the paper is held to the light / The mark shows through / Ripples appear round your feet / Yet you refuse to walk on water / In the offices of the city the workers wade through political treacle / Loneliness is soaked into the floors / Runs down the walls / You can feel it / In the tightness of the fist / The pressure on the pen / The slamming of the phone / The crease in the shirt collar / The clip-clop of high heels / The rip in the tights / The scratch on the Gucci sunglasses / The Post-its plastered on screens / The twist of the paper clip / The hum of the printer / The over-sharpened pencil.

It's in the hole punch / The staple gun / The soulless PowerPoint presentation / The despise at the sign hanging on the boss's door / It's in the tone of the voice / The doodle on the notepad / Scribbled in the board meeting / The secretary cheating / The overloaded briefcase / The tick of the taxi meter.

You can't hide a heart that lies and leaks / Like air from an inner tube / Relationships breakdown / Economic structures fail / Planets disappear from the system.

was it just the moon pulling me out of shape that wanted me to rip my face off?

We are on a mission to kiss the sun / To scorch our lips / Singe our fingertips / Blister our eyes / On the fire pit in the sky / We will melt and blacken our platinum rings / Walk hand in hand into solar storms / Move close enough to the searing heat to hear the crackle of bone and the spit of thunder / Close enough to feel our heartstrings snapping in the flame / Close enough to hear the glow of the sun's ray / Close enough to hear the corona cry / To hear its magnetic wind weep gently / Close enough to scoop up the sun's rage and freeze it in test tubes.

We will keep going even though this mission is impossible / It's a journey no real human can make / Like watching hot embers dance into the night / A split second and they are gone.

To make it we'll need to change direction / Use the gravity of Venus to slow us down / Like a handbrake turn in a farmer's field in late summer.

There are so many stars to kiss / Yet some think the world is flat / Whilst others build machines to fly to the edge of the solar system and beyond / There is not an engineer alive who could conceive a structure strong enough or wide enough to bridge the gap between their thoughts.

We are so close to the sun that we cannot see the night sky / We cannot see the stars / So we cannot read and shed light on our own story / Did we learn nothing from Icarus?

This poem had to be rebuilt because it crash-landed into a swimming pool and all the words were lost.

'Close enough to hit sixes into the sun.' This line never made the final poem but I really like it.

loneliness is a wild horse in a science lab
reduced to bacteria growing in a Petri dish
a metal spade scraping the hard dirt of your inside
a common sadness
a shared aloneness
did we invent it?

When Wonder Died

There was a twin tower
There was a bird flying overhead
There was a phone call to say that you were dead
There was a body lying on the bed
There was a stiff drink
Then another one.
And another one.
Another one.
Another.
Anoth.
Anot.
Ano.
An.
A.
.

There was another morning waking up alone.

It's Lonely On This Wall

loneliness is a river flowing over a rock
you are the rock
loneliness is the river
you are isolated in the shallows
but the river just keeps coming

Neptune

I watch my life like a steam train crashing into the sea

I had some grit in my eye / So I went to the medicine cabinet to find the eye-bath cup to wash out the dirt / I filled the small cup with water and placed it onto my eye / I blinked several times to try to remove the grit / Whatever was in there was lodged in tightly / I blinked more vigorously / Out came the small piece of grit / I blinked again / Out came a whole stone / Then a rock / Then a rock pool / A shrimp / An edible crab (the one I had crushed a long time ago during a family holiday) / Then came a jellyfish / And an octopus / Then a whole shoreline full of seaweed / Longshore drift / Flotsam and jetsam / Plastic bottles / The carcasses of sea birds and rotting fish bones / A broken disused jetty / Dolphins / Basking sharks / Blue whales / Eventually I rinsed away the tears that had been lodged in the corner of my eye all my life / The sharpest clearest white sky appeared / I could finally see again.

I love those skies that look like other worlds
alien harbours containing burning seas of pink and orange
and red
surrounded by blue and silver wisps and whisks of cloud
like distant mountain ranges and blistering craters

I wonder if I flew towards them
whether I could ever reach them

Horizon

a hem of dress

a hippo's back

the ripple-wingbeat of a bee

the melting honey

the lovers' sunset

a mountain view

a cratered moon

a duvet at dawn

a swollen-eye sky

swaddled in Earth's blue blanket

We Welcomed The Spring

it was white wine and cigarettes between courses
in a restaurant we could hardly afford
we spoke our blistered minds
how we'd been falling and failing upwards all our lives
trying to fit in
succeeding
waving
drowning
like a wasp in a Coke can
hitting the sides
sucking up the sugar
wings sodden with thick syrup
fake pollen pulling us down
belly-up in carbonate
floating on fizz
in a metal mew

the fair had come to town
the Cinderella gown girls ride waltzers
lose slippers on chairoplanes
and their virginity behind funhouses and sideshow tents
we'd fling ping-pongs in bowls to win goldfish
watch them slowly suffocate in plastic bags
then head on home
luminous green candyfloss and hotdogs in hand

within a week the fair had left town
the goldfish turned upside down
met their fate
met their calling
dying belly-up
it's their way of falling

Death is... *tick correct box

a)   wooden furniture floating in underwater apartments ☐

b)   a sentence on a bonfire clogging the air with smoke ☐

c)   a pink-ribbed sky ☐

d)   an unmanned Uber drone delivering parcels to your door ☐

e)   a road with the cats eyes dug out ☐

f)   none of the above ☐

g)   all of the above ☐

Mermaid

you always hear the stories
how Dave the Fish
or Five Bellies Bob
or Crazy Leg Richardson
or any of those small-time crooks
would fill your boots with concrete
throw you head-first from the nearest jetty
if you made the wrong move

I wonder what she did to deserve her shrimp-food fate
who is the girl bathed in plankton light?
the boss's unfaithful wife?
a double agent?
a high-class hooker?
a mermaid out of her depth?

the bees swarm round her head
reading underwater signals
whilst breathing through reed snorkels

every soldier and sailor
tailor and tinker
fall for her charms
hook line and sinker

the stars beat in your heart
the heart simmers in the night sky
and it always will
till the day you die

Make-Believe Mermaid

beads balance on Adam's ale
a sailor's seasick tale
forsaken fisherman's thoughts
flecked on the bosom of make-believe mermaids
angel dots
pearls of polished light

yarn spinner
cotton fibber
tale twister
tide turner

burning hands in iced salt water
as fairy drops drift
brake
undulate
on shallow sun-drenched tsunami dreams

In The Changing Rooms Of The Local Swimming Pool

I like swimming in a pool
as opposed to life
because unlike life there is a side to hold onto when you are out
of your depth
and you can clearly see the bottom
and the end

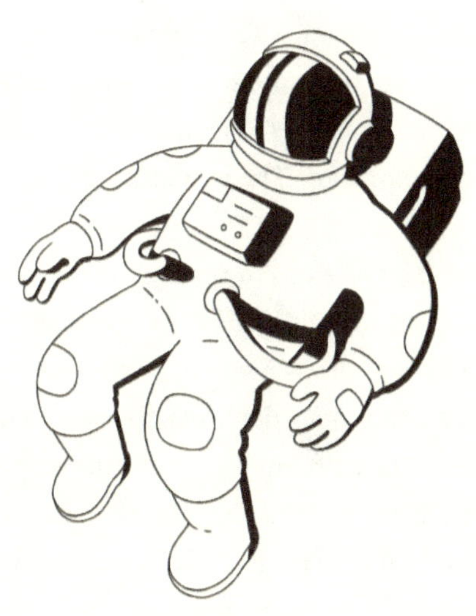

Crowded Swimming Baths

It is a busy swimming pool / I know those echoes and squeals / Kids all bombing around and shivering / Chlorine-drenched / I can swim but the instructors haunt my stroke / I am scared of them because they will make me jump from the diving board / And I'm scared of heights / But they bellow and scream / And my toes curl over the edge of the board / And the tears tiptoe on the edge of my eye / As I try hopelessly to hold them in / The tears and fear pour out / And I do not dive in ever / Never ever / Again.

I feel the same pain when my dad takes me onto the roof of Tesco to clean the windows / I'm scared / I feel like I am swimming / Or drowning / Or waving / There are people pissing in this pool out of fear / That is why your eyes are stinging / It's the chlorine reacting with all the piss / The more they sting the more piss there is / The more fear / The more hidden tears in the shower.

Although sunlight streams in through the large glass windows it seems dim and distant in this space / In the deep end / The bottom of the pool drops away from one and a half metres to four metres / The echoes don't reach down that far / I know / I touched the tiles with my hand / Retrieved my dreams from the bottom / Held my breath and my dreams for as long as possible / Until I had to push off from the floor to quickly break the surface / To fill my lungs with oxygen / To come up for air.

We are made to lie down on the pool's edge to practise our stroke / The tiles are dirty and covered in hair and cold puddles of pool water / The amount of water I've swallowed makes me sick / And I hold onto the edge tightly until the shouts and bellows come / To "Go!" / To "Swim!" / To "Kick!" / "Harder!" / "Faster!" / They're not teaching you to swim / They are training you for life / This is how they want you to survive.

The changing rooms are a bare-knuckle fight / Don't show any weakness / Hold your towel tight around your waist whilst pulling down your trunks / So no goon can tug it away / So the mob cannot pile into your manhood / Whilst an array of wet towels spun into whips fly your way / It is brutal / But you have to endure it if you're the runt of the group or an easy target.

I'd throw wet tissue on the ceiling so it stuck / This would encourage the idiots to join in / Keep them occupied / Take their minds off attacking the weaker members of the group / Your mouth can get you into trouble and out of it depending on how the dice fall / I remember the heat / It was stifling / I hated it.

In the night / The water that was trapped in your ear trickles onto your pillow / Clearing your throat and your thoughts.

Jesus walked the waves
left footprints dancing on the surface
and ever since we've skimmed the surf's scalp
pierced the pond's periphery
peered inside liquid veneer
a Polaroid void
an endless eyeless carcass
a blind corpse

waves weigh heavy
on submerged and sunken sea dogs
sub human
sub marine
sad marine

my pining pirate
Blackbeard blues blinker
sinless Long John Silver
sorrowful seafarer sailor
weeping weed and whale
to glide on tearful tide

we are lost at sea
lugging a bag of serpent bones
to voiceless echoed groans

ogle goggle and gander
kiss a watery skin
head down in drink
we glimpse our forlorn unborn tomorrows
wrecked on seabed

The small boy jumped into the pool without his armbands /
He was drowning / I jumped into the pool fully clothed to save
him / I thought his mum would appreciate this / My phone was
in my pocket / I lost all the poems I had written on my phone
and hadn't backed up / I wrote this poem to replace the ones I
had lost / I'm not sure it was worth it / Maybe I should have let
the small boy drown / But he was my son and he wasn't covered
by the insurance / And I wasn't even entitled to an upgrade / It
turned out it was also cheaper to invest in another phone rather
than another human being both financially and emotionally.

Poem By Bill Aged Four

I have water in my eye
is it a river?

Soul Erosion

the television in the doctor's surgery
is advertising illnesses
"do you have this illness?"

it's an epidemic
the World Health Organisation said so
everybody is getting one

it is easy to forget how to breathe
it is easy to forget how to be human
like how water forgets how to freeze
though I can't imagine water forgets how to flow

but I've seen a river straighten
a river that has forgotten how to meander
how it aches to be an oxbow lake

The tap has been dripping for so long that a stalactite has appeared on the very tip of the spout where the water drips out / The dripping nose of the tap / Stalactite snot / I know it is a stalactite because my nan told me that tights are pulled down / Tights can be pulled up too though Nan! / She is not here to clip me round the ear.

What is the spout bit of a tap called?

It's a tap. Just a tap. The on-off valve and the short pipe is called a tap.

But that's like saying an elephant's trunk is just called an elephant and not a trunk.

What's the trunk part of the tap called?

Can't just be a tap. That's a bit like saying I'm a human but I don't have a nose or a hand or a heart or a head. They are all just human.

Hope is...

a)   a cloud fossilised in stone   ☐

b)   a cricket match played on an empty beach
        with stumps made out of sand   ☐

c)   a stingray swimming in an ocean of plastic or
        a plastic ocean with some salt water added   ☐

d)   a group of students discussing whether it
        is a poem or whether it is prose   ☐

e)   none of the above   ☐

f)   all of the above   ☐

clouds

fall

down

when

you

hang

on

to

them

imagine if all the world was wine
and every step you took
your bare feet
pressed and crushed
ripened grape

I have enough / I have enough food to eat / I have enough water /
I have enough space / I have enough love / I have enough pain /
It's important that it is there / It reminds me how to laugh / And
to know I am laughing / The two are very close together / I have
enough laughter / I have enough loneliness.

Have you ever laughed when you are alone?

if you're good at admin you will do well in life

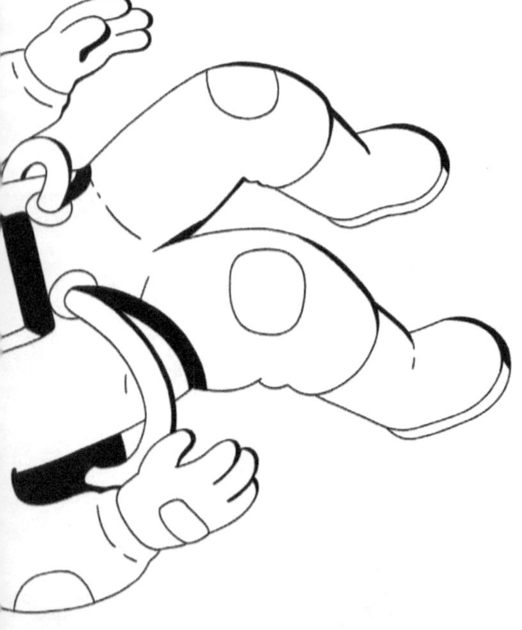

count every penny
know the price of the sky
make your own coffin
lie in it
wait to die

do you have enough money to live?
do you have enough money to cry?
measure up your own coffin
lie in it
wait to die

my time on Earth
I never became a member
I only signed in as a guest

Life Without You

blossom bloom
blossom moss
blossom fall
blossom loss
blossom less
that is life without you
I guess

after ever

they lived happily

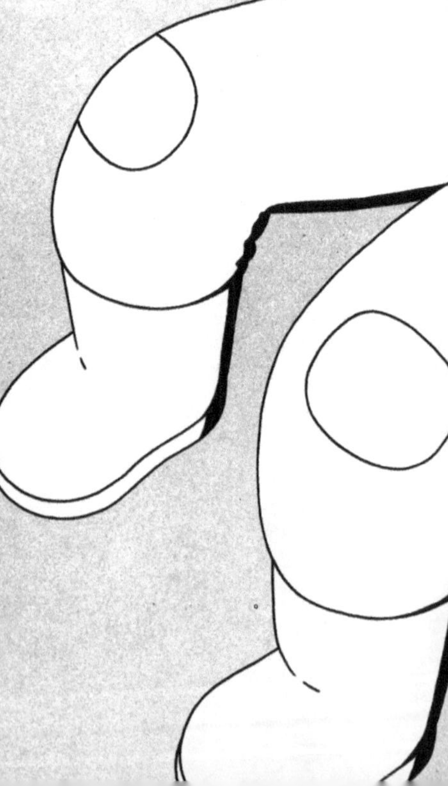

Index of Titles / *First Lines*

Previously appeared:

- **What is Emptiness?** first appeared in Made In Spode by Katya de Grunwald (Piper Press, 2015)

- **We Didn't Know It Was Called Hip-Hop (Part 1)** was written and performed for RAP Party at Southbank Centre, curated by Inua Ellams (2015)

- **We Didn't Know It Was Called Hip-Hop (Part 2)** was written and performed for RAP Party at Shoreditch House, curated by Inua Ellams (2016)

- **The Road To Wigan Casino** first appeared in Double Bill: Poems Inspired By Popular Culture, edited by Andy Jackson (Red Squirrel Press, 2014)

- **When My World Was Turned** first appeared in Pie and Papier-Mâché (Trinovantes, 2007)

- **Pebble** first appeared in Pie and Papier-Mâché (Trinovantes, 2007)

- **The Most Beautiful Man In The World** first appeared in Pie and Papier-Mâché (Trinovantes, 2007)

- **Retail Therapy** first appeared in Pie and Papier-Mâché (Trinovantes, 2007)

- **Life Without You** first appeared in Pie and Papier-Mâché (Trinovantes, 2007)

Acknowledgements

Thank you, Damien Weighill, for your amazing skills and patience. Thank you, Hope Nicholson, for correcting the wrongs and standing up for the rights. Thank you, Clive Birnie, Bridget Hart, Harriet Evans and Burning Eye, for your ongoing support. Thank you, AF Harrold and Deanna Rodger, for your incredibly kind words and support over the years. Thank you to everyone who took part in the live test readings, especially Clair Whitefield, Gemma Rogers and Paul Cree. Thank you to my Bang Said The Gun team, especially Martin Galton, Rob Auton and Laurie Bolger, for creating some very special moments. A very big thank you to the Arts Council England and especially to Sarah Sanders and Layla Wolfson. Without your support and encouragement this project would have not been possible. And thank you to everyone who has ever bought or read one of my books or purchased a ticket to a show I was involved in. It means so much.

Thank you. All my love. Big hugs.

x dan x

www.ingramcontent.com/pod-product-compliance
Lightning Source LLC
Chambersburg PA
CBHW032007050726
47590CB00006B/2082